SCHOOL
LIBRARY
SERVICE

Forests

By John Wood

BookLife

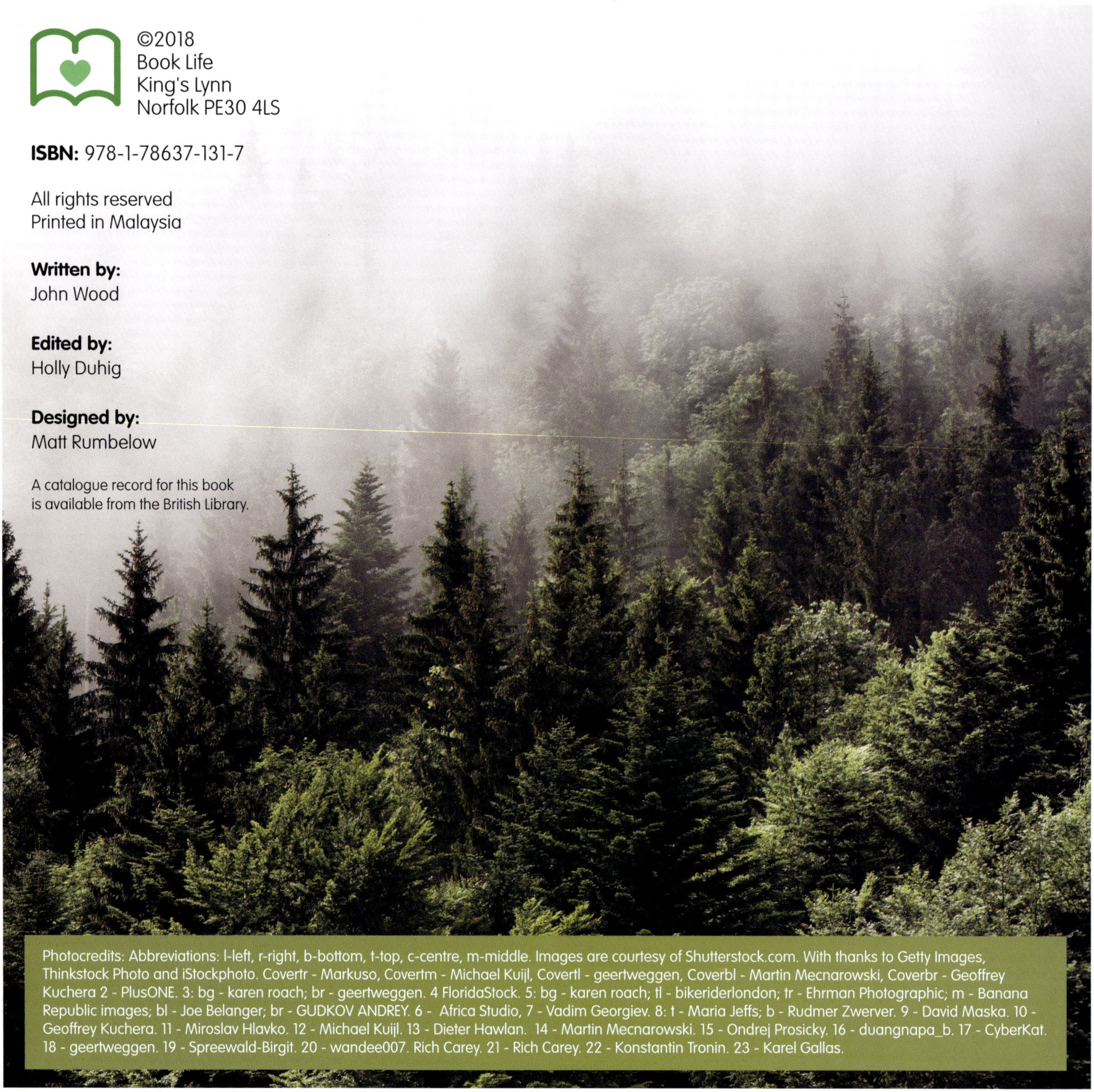

©2018
Book Life
King's Lynn
Norfolk PE30 4LS

ISBN: 978-1-78637-131-7

Written by:
John Wood

Edited by:
Holly Duhig

Designed by:
Matt Rumbelow

A catalogue record for this book
is available from the British Library.

CONTENTS

Words that look like this can be found in the glossary on page 24.

WHAT IS A HABITAT?

A habitat is a place where an animal lives. It provides the animal with food, **shelter** and everything else it needs to survive.

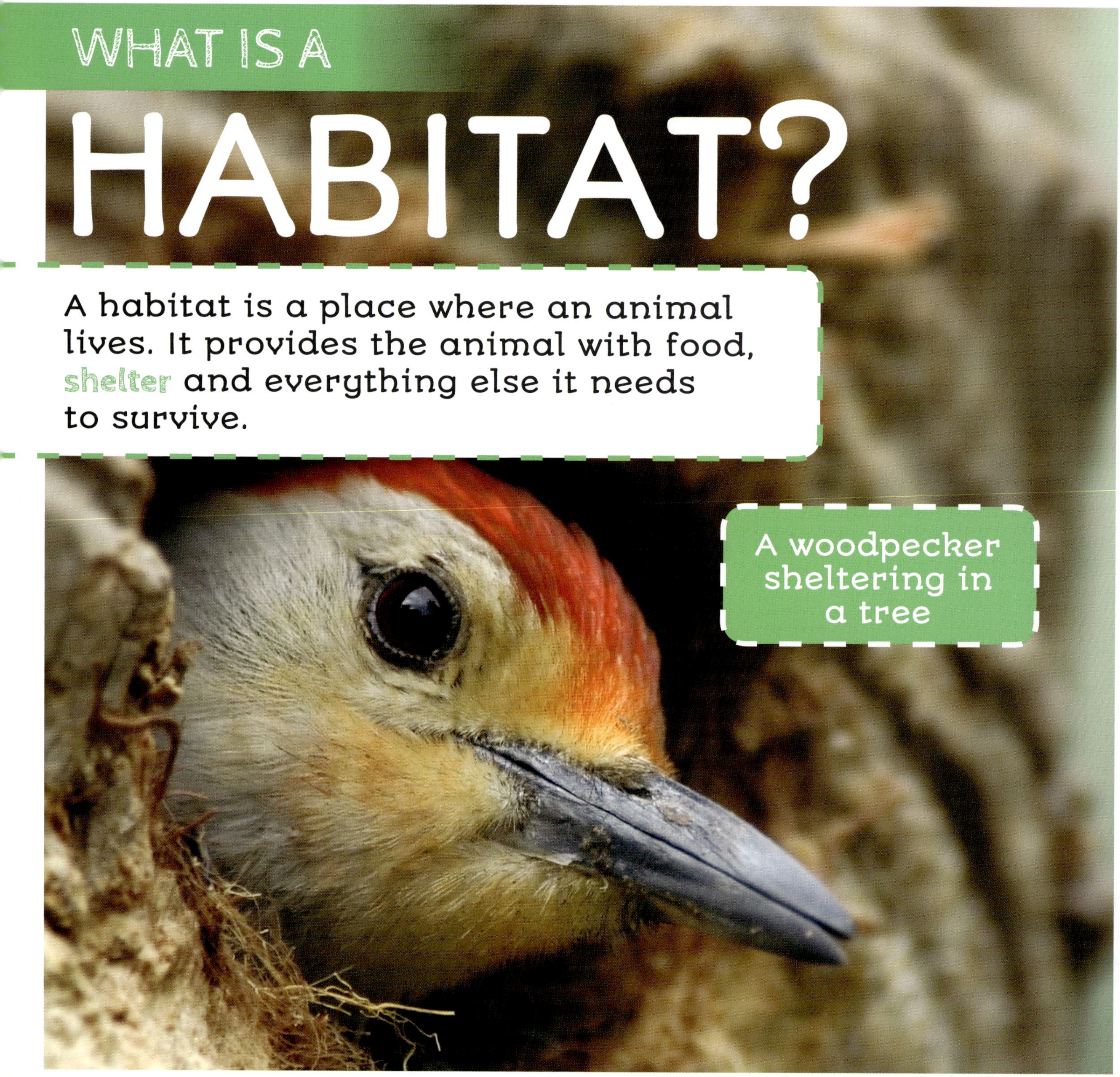

A woodpecker sheltering in a tree

There are lots of different habitats in the world. Each one is home to many different animals.

Forests

Grasslands

Deserts

Oceans

Jungles

WHAT IS A FOREST?

A forest is a type of habitat that is covered in plants and trees. Forests are often found in places that experience all four seasons.

Summer

Autumn

Winter

Spring

Some forests have trees that shed their leaves in winter. Other forests have trees that keep their leaves all year round. These are called evergreen trees.

Evergreen Trees

FOREST HABITAT

Forests are home to many different animal habitats. The trees in forests provide homes for many animals, as does the forest floor.

Forests in places with lots of hills might also have caves. Caves provide animals with shelter and make great animal homes.

FOXES

Foxes make **burrows** in the forest floor. A fox's burrow is called a den. They sleep and look after their **young** in their dens.

A young fox is called a kit.

Foxes like to make their dens in dry, sandy soil. The entrance to a fox's den is very small but, as it goes deeper, the den becomes wider.

Kits in a den

BEARS

Bears make the whole forest their home. From towering trees to forest streams, there are no parts of the forest that bears won't explore!

Bears make dens underground or use caves as their homes. They sleep in their homes during the cold winter months. This is called hibernation.

WOODPECKERS

Woodpeckers get their name from the way they peck at the side of trees with their long beaks. They do this to find insects to eat.

Woodpeckers also make their homes by pecking holes into trees. These holes are called woodpecker nests.

Woodpeckers can peck 20 times per second!

BATS

Bats' homes are called roosts. Bats make their roosts in all sorts of places, especially in caves and trees. When bats settle in their roosts, it is called roosting.

Bats sleep upside down in their roosts.

When female bats have babies, they roost in warmer places such as tree hollows. Here, the bat and her baby are sheltered from the wind.

A bat in a tree hollow

SQUIRRELS

Squirrels also make their homes in trees. During the winter, they make dens in tree hollows. They fill these with moss and leaves for extra warmth.

In warmer weather, squirrels make nests called dreys. They are made out of twigs, grass and dry leaves. They make dreys in the branches of trees.

A squirrel in its drey

FORESTS IN
DANGER

People cut down the trees in forests and use the wood to make things such as paper, furniture and even houses. When lots of trees in a forest get cut down, it is called deforestation.

Deforestation

Deforestation makes animal habitats smaller and destroys many animal homes. Without their homes, it is hard for these animals to survive. When animals find it hard to survive, they are said to be endangered.

RED WOLVES

Red wolves are endangered because their habitat is being destroyed by deforestation. Because of deforestation, there is less space for red wolves to find food.

RED PANDAS

Red pandas make their homes high up in trees. They are also endangered because people are cutting down their homes.

GLOSSARY

beaks the hard, pointed mouths of birds

burrows holes or tunnels dug by animals

endangered in danger of dying out

hollows small holes or grooves, usually in trees

moss a small, green plant that grows in damp habitats

shelter protection from danger and harsh weather

soil the upper layer of earth in which plants grow

young an animal's offspring

Index